Endorsements

"Gina's poetic account of her inner journey recounts seasons of dysfunction, forgiveness, healing, rebuilding, and empowerment. This is a personal and poignant labour of love, a generous offering of advice for anyone travelling a similar road."

DONNA YOUNGDAHL

"Gina's candor, her generous and loving nature, as well as her undeniable strength of character shine through every single page of this insightful recount of her own blended family's story. Her poetic style of writing pulls us in as readers and captures our hearts. For anyone whose family's story is anything but normal... and that would be most people in these modern times... this is a story of courage, of love, and of faith."

JANIQUE HÉBERT

"Blended families can be a challenge at best. Gina DeBrincat draws from her own life experience, from personal trials and triumphs of living and managing a blended family, to bring us a handbook of essentials to make this family dynamic work. Her spirited personality shines through each of her words and sentences. She has, with wit, wisdom and creativity, laid out a blueprint for a strong foundation on which to build a healthy and thriving blended family dynamic.

Sometimes the best way to find a solution to a challenge before us is to listen to the advice of someone who has walked the same or similar journey. If you are facing the challenges of a blended family, these pages will encourage and inspire you. It is a must read. Thank you, Gina, for opening your heart to us and sharing your journey with such generosity."

ROSALIE RATTAI

Matrix of the Blended Family

Gina DeBrincat

MATRIX OF THE BLENDED FAMILY

Unless otherwise indicated, all Scripture quotations are taken from the New American Standard Bible®, Copyright © 1960, 1962, 1963, 1971, 1972, 1973, 1975, 1977, 1995 by The Lockman Foundation. Used by permission.

Scripture quotations marked MSG are taken from The Message. Copyright © 1993, 1994, 1995, 1996, 2000, 2001, 2002. Used by permission of NavPress Publishing Group. Scripture quotations marked AMP are taken from the Amplified Bible, Copyright © 1954, 1958, 1962, 1964, 1965, 1987 by The Lockman Foundation. Used by permission. All rights reserved.

ISBN-13: 978-1-926676-67-8

Printed in Canada.

Printed by Word Alive Press
131 Cordite Road, Winnipeg, MB R3W 1S1
www.wordalivepress.ca

Mixed Sources
Cert no. SW-COC-001271
© 1996 FSC

This book is dedicated
to my family,

MY HUSBAND MARK,
AND MY CHILDREN
JEN, AISHA, PASCAL, AND JEFFREY

who taught me to approach life with patience and
hope, fired by love.

AND

to all the blended families who bravely
endeavour to make a go of it.

FOREWORD

Sharing in Gina's life and story through her writings has been enriching and very thought provoking.

Gina and I have been in and out of each other's lives now for many years as sisters in Christ, but especially as friends… long before she was married. I read this book in one sitting. My first response was "Oh Lord, I didn't know." The impact of this overwhelmed me for a moment, even days after.

The Matrix of the Blended Family is not just for those who have had to deal with separation, divorces, and all the fragmentation of hearts and lives that it entails; it is for all of us. For those going through crisis and those walking with friends who are hurting—this book brings life and hope in a fresh and amazing way.

Gina shows us how something can break, seem to be totally lost, and the miracle of restoration that brings a 'blending' to a 'bonding' as only the Lord can do when He is given first place in the process.

This is a timely book and one to share with anyone who is touched by the tragedy of loss in marriage and family relationships.

HELEN TOEWS
Award-winning Author of "Emma's Corner" and
"Supernatural Childbirth"

ACKNOWLEDGEMENTS

Father, Son and Holy Spirit, for imparting their courage.

Mark DeBrincat, for his constant support and help in making time for me to write.

Jennifer Bertrand, for all the life lessons we had together.

Aisha Toupin, for her sensitivity and creativity.

Pascal Toupin, for his thoughtful and artful heart.

Jeffrey DeBrincat, for his humour and perspective.

Brenda Carriere, for her "around the clock" care.

Mr. Scaletta, who told me I'd "never have a flare for English."

Simone Morin, for her daily prayers for my family's life.

TABLE OF CONTENTS

SPRING

SUMMER

INTRODUCTION

The blended family was not my initial experience of the family. I grew up with my biological mother and father, four siblings, and a dog. We were a typical "old-fashioned" family who went to church, said grace before dinner, fought and argued yet loved each other deeply. Even though there may have been cause for divorce, the word was never spoken or even thought of as an experience that could take place in our family, and it did not.

It was me who introduced such a notion into my own personal family. I married a divorced man, who had a beautiful little daughter. Divorce and the blended family were the two birds I hit with one stone. And so began my journey into "the new family of the twenty-first century."

But I did not stop there. Thirteen years, two more children, and much heartache later, my husband left. I then wore the hat of a divorced, single mother to my two biological children and the single stepmother to my stepdaughter. And so began my continued journey into "the newer family of the twenty-first century."

But I was on a roll, so… I met and married my present husband, the love of my life, who had never been married before but had a son. Now I wore the hats of a divorced/remarried mother of two, stepmother of two, and first wife of one. And so continues my journey of labour and love in the present "newest family of the twenty-first century."

Prologue

The sun shines somewhere far above the hazy, grey blanket of cloud. While I cannot see it or feel its warmth, I know that its light is actually shining brightly. I have experienced it, as I am sure you have, up in a plane. On ascent, you climb through wind and clouds and rain only to burst through the weather into the gleaming, bright sun. During the day, it is always shining. We just do not always feel it or see it. But it is there. If it were not, there would be no light, no life.

In writing this book, I have needed to remember the sun. Embarking, for the first time, into the realm of writing a book, I want to believe that the thoughts and words are always close at hand, even if they are not channelling through me, at that very moment. If I climb up through the weathers of my life, I will once again experience the surge of the words that I feel have been given to me to write. If they can dance wildly and freely, but with divine purpose, I believe I will pull forth the words to fill the pages of this book. By daily putting my nose to the grindstone, in whatever task I am challenged with, I will get what I patiently wait for.

We will take a seasonal look at the chapters of this book.

The first section will aptly depict the season of autumn. The leaves on the trees wither and fall to the ground only to make room for another crop, in another time. The death and dying process is a catharsis in the blended family.

The winter brings the test of our efforts. The snow, wind, and harsh temperatures challenge our very existence and demonstrate to us what we are truly made of. These chapters will specifically tackle the struggle and survival techniques necessary for the winter months.

Following, of course, is spring, with its promise of renewed life, strength, and hope. Spring desperately tries to come forth, but we are not certain that it will bloom until it actually does. It is here that we release the energy to carry on.

And then the warm and gentle breezes of the summer blow in, where success, significance, and satisfaction thrive and flourish in the blended family.

The constantly revolving circles of the seasons we encounter in the blended family do not follow a prearranged order, as they are executed in nature. They sprout up in our families as the need arises and in their perfect time. It never ceases to involve us in its constant revolutions.

So in the following pages, the words are given and written and read. The seasonal story will unfold. But the most satisfying thing for me is that summer *does* come. As you continue on in these pages, you will live out the seasons of your own blended family.

AUTUMN

"In our sleep, pain that cannot forget falls
drop by drop upon the heart and in our own
despair, against our will, comes wisdom
through the awful grace of God."
AESCHYLUS

ONE

THE GREAT DIVIDE

I sat motionless… emotionless… staring out at the swelling waters of the Red River. The water, creeping close to my feet, had spread far beyond its banks. The sandbags did not deter or deflect its forceful nature. Nothing could tame the water that year. It just defied the rules and roamed at will. Its course had been set and no efforts would cause a retreat. There was no turning back for the river. It was exploding onto the land and drowning everything in its path. Somehow, at that moment, understanding that the waters were rushing over their boundaries into places that they should not be, I knew that my marriage, too, was now rushing over its borders into places it should not be. Stung by this thought, I noticed that the river carried remnants of people's lives in its currents and I could finally let my own memories of a life I once lived be carried away by my own tears. In the midst of the clear and terrible revelation that my marriage was ending, I had resigned myself to the "great divide."

I felt alone. I was alone, except for a deep and approaching sense of peace and hope that surrounded me. It was strange, but I think it was a type of 'knowing' that the pending end of my marriage, even though I did not want divorce, was an inevitable and unavoidable thing. In the previous two years, I had done all I could to save my marriage. I had talked about it, prayed about it, fought for it, cried for it, tried to ignore it, sacrificed for it, blamed myself for it, sought counselling for it, and slugged it out for my children's sake. But the time had finally come. It was finished. In accepting this final fact, a sense of peace rushed through me. It was relief, finally, to see a light of deliverance from such a tender state of being. But more than that, this peace brought a renewed promise of better things to come. Hope, to me that day, meant a new start. After having done everything I knew to do to bring reconciliation, a new start meant washing my hands of this present situation and moving on. And I have always been a firm believer that hope never disappoints.

And so it was the effects of the great flood of 1997 that seemed to "wash that man right out of my hair" and my head was clear to carry on and raise my family.

The Great Divide

"When you feel as if your grip is slipping
and you can't hold on any longer, just tie a
knot in the end of the rope and hang on
some more. Help is on the way."
GINA'S JOURNAL # 4

TWO

FAMILY: BREAK IT DOWN

"Humpty Dumpty sat on a wall,
Humpty Dumpty had a great fall.
All the King's horses and all the King's men
Couldn't put Humpty together again."
AUTHOR UNKNOWN

This little nursery rhyme is symbolic of the signs of our times. It has strong cultural significance today and it is in keeping with the grim and grotesque storylines of the nursery rhymes we recite to our children.

To be fair and politically correct, in our analogy, Humpty could indeed be a man or a woman. And what does Humpty first of all do? He or she 'sat on a wall.' Humpty sits on the proverbial fence, not fully committing to a marriage, to anyone, or to anything—possibly not even bothering to publicly state and commit to the intent of union, by marriage, by simply "living together." But it is crucial here to mention that even in the context of marriage, the attitude and intent of the heart could also be less implicated. The door is deliberately left ajar in order to accommodate an easy way out, if in fact it doesn't work itself out. Whether this is a first, second or third union, this non-committed approach is destructive to the two adults and to the biological or stepchildren involved. Since there is little moral code or standard of behaviour set forth in this type of togetherness, anything goes. It is the perfect platform for deep hurt, disappointment, and failure of a broken family.

By not committing to another person from the depths of your heart and by a sense of deep conviction, we enable each other to do what comes naturally. Therein lies the rub. Left to our own devices, by not positioning ourselves to be accountable to anything or anyone, we will naturally make a selfish choice. We do it because it feels good. We do it because we deserve to be happy. We do it because we are entitled to make our own choices. We do it for our own sanity. We do it because there is no other choice. We do it because it is our right. We do it because we are not treated adequately. And my personal favourite, we do it because we have somehow or other fallen out of love. We clutch all of our reasons close to our hearts, but this type of reckoning darkens our family life, because family life is an unselfish and giving one. The attitude in family life flows out of a commitment to the partners and children you have joined your life to. If this is not your style, Humpty, then you shouldn't be climbing this wall!

The front door entrance to a union is a wedding and all the trimmings. This publicly announces to your future spouse, your friends, your family, and your children and/or stepchildren that you are committed. The back door entrance to a union is living together. This announces to your future spouse, friends, family, and your children and/or stepchildren that you are just trying it out to see if it fits your desired lifestyle. The bedroom window entrance to a union announces to your "use-as needed" lover, friends, family, and your children and/or stepchildren that your interest in this partner is exclusively for your own fleeting pleasure. So Humpty Dumpty sits on the fence!

All of this sets us up for the fall. If we are not committed to a relationship and/or a family of people, we will ultimately fail them and destroy these relationships.

> "The primary commitment is to making this new marriage work. That needs to be stated out loud by both husband and wife to each other and then shared with all the children involved. Obviously, making a marriage work is easier said than done, but it needs to be said

before it can be done. This notification also closes the exit doors that offer escape when times get tough. Working on building and growing our blended family will be like training for a marathon run. When we start training, the task before us looks highly improbable except for the fact that others have done what we are about to start doing. After a few months of training, we begin to feel comfortable in our program and begin to really believe we can do this race when race day comes in six months. Building a blended family is like this, except the finish line really only comes when we die. (...) That's a personal commitment that every man and woman in a blended family needs to think through."

—JIM SMOKE (*7 Keys to a Healthy Blended Family*)

To all the members of a family, being committed means being there, being present. Not just physically present, but spiritually, emotionally and psychologically present. Not just on weekends and special holidays, but making and taking in all the daily-grind activities, problems and joys. As a result of our thoughts, intents and deeds, we respond accordingly. Where we allow our mind to linger, our soul and body will, before long, want to live. Sooner or later, in a non-committed situation, we fall. Commitment is like glue, but glue is not used to fix everything. Marriage and commitment is not for everyone. It is important to search your heart before you enter in. But I believe it is imperative for us individually to make our intentions clear or we could end up in a lifelong mess, dragging the people we love through it.

Please note that the following statements are strictly from my own observation and experience. They unquestionably do not reflect the fundamental nature of the laws and services that we have in place. However, I have found that these systems fall short of meeting the needs of the people dealing with divorce, remarriage, and all the children who are impacted by it. Our "king's men" cannot put us back together again. Our laws and precepts do not enable this putting back together thing. The laws of our land make it simple and easy to get out. And we get to foot the bill, in more ways than one! Our lawyers help us to separate, annul divorce, restrain, and order our lives according to what we want or what we feel we need. We begin, or continue as is sometimes the case, to use our children as pawns to get what we want and what we feel we need. None of it helps our children. We have believed the lie that "children are resilient." Well, this is most assuredly not true. Children simply do not have the mental facility to outwardly express their pain and suffering at the hands of the adults in their lives. It is nearly impossible for them to even try to begin to comprehend the kind of turmoil they are experiencing as a result of their parents' thoughts, feelings, decisions, and actions. They are not able to discern the source of the pain that we put them through, and therefore are unable to put it into words and let us know what they are experiencing. But our children feel every pang and every twinge of anger, separation, divorce, remarriage, new siblings, new homes, and new schools. They had no input into the ripping apart of their families. Since the family is supposed to be the stable factor in their lives, how do we expect they are going to feel?

It is our children that require someone to help them sort it all out and understand that it is not their fault. They need to be given constructive methods in order to assist them to put their own selves back together again. Who better than the committed parents know what is the best solution for the sake of the children? Even though the children live in two separate households, the parents still have the daunting task of raising them, separately. Because the parents do not agree on much, in this situation, the challenges become almost insurmountable. The mediators and social service workers try desperately to help us. We attend classes and workshops which teach us how to respond with the sake of the children in mind. But if we are not committed in the first place and do not have these strategies in place while we are a family, once the family has broken down, how can we possible work together and put these tactics in place, after the fact? In a high conflict situation, this is nearly impossible. It is called a high conflict situation for a very good reason!

> "The family is the cornerstone of our society. More than any other force it shapes the attitude, the hopes, the ambitions, and the values of the child. And when the family collapses, it is the children that are usually damaged. When it happens on a mass scale the community itself is crippled."
>
> —PRESIDENT LYNDON B. JOHNSON

We throw our kids to the wolves when we insist on our own way. Not only do we *not* want to make our own bed, we do not even want to sleep in it. Our laws and programs work for this end. And we pay them dearly to do it for us. We put no price on our own freedom.

The programs of our social systems have their terms put in place for very good and well thought out reasons. They are based on helping and meeting the needs of the masses. However, in my humble opinion and from my experience, a very important piece has been omitted. This piece represents the specific needs of each individual family and the basic needs of the human spirit. We have forgotten the human element in our quest to get to the end of the lines of people waiting for help. Our social programs are designed in the best manner possible, but they are flawed and fail us. For my family, personal counselling, both emotional and spiritual, with and for each individual, was the key to understanding our present circumstances and taking the appropriate measures to get through the mess.

The proof of the pudding is still evident to this present day. We are constantly using the counselling tools we have been given. Had we not taken these steps, of our own accord, and followed them diligently, we may not be where we are today. If we are to succeed in these matters, healing of the soul needs to take place. This deep and lasting kind of healing is not a quick fix so you can get on with life. Where there is change, there is conflict and loss. Conflict and loss cannot be ignored. It will not just go away or be healed by the passing of time. The human soul must be attended to, cared for, nurtured, and healed. You can not sweep this under the carpet. If unattended or mistreated, this conflict will inevitably wait for you and someday, even years away, blast you in the face and harshly surface in your life. We never truly move forward until we have faced our demons and cast them out. Until such a time as this, they hover around us, waiting for a moment to bite and devour. Please, for your sake and especially for the sake of the children, take the time, effort, and energy to heal your souls. The curing of the soul must be sought out in the proper places. We have a long way to go and must travel this road in humility and selflessness. I believe, with the proper attitude, we could actually do it.

But for the present time, Humpty stays broken and carries on with his emotionally and spiritually damaged life.

Ours is a sad state of affairs.

"Humpty Dumpty sat on a wall,
Humpty Dumpty had a great fall,
All the King's horses and all the King's men,
Couldn't put Humpty together again."

And this is no yolk!

THREE

LIKE A BRIDGE OVER
TROUBLED WATER

What is wrong with me? Am I not a good enough wife? Am I not a good enough mother? Am I not a good enough cook? Am I not a good enough housekeeper? Am I not a good enough lover? Do I not make enough money? Am I too fat? Am I too thin? Why am I missing the mark on everything I touch? What is it? What is wrong with me?

If you sincerely ask yourself these questions and you can find no adequate answer, please know that the problem is not with you! Stop second-guessing yourself. To engage in such soul-searching and to never find a solution means there is something desperately wrong with the relationship. Where there are two people, there are two stories, two messages, two sets of feelings, and no *one* is to blame. Fault, in this setting, is always shared. But I said all that to say this: sometimes, in a relationship between two people, toxicity festers. The toxic person wants to be free of any responsibility whatsoever. So they blame everything on the other and punctuate the fault, in hopes that their partner will actually believe they are to blame. If they can achieve this twist in the truth, then they have effectively alleviated any accountability for themselves. If we are not growing in a positive manner and encouraging each other to good works, we do not remain neutral. We are not like vehicles that can idle in neutral, go forward, or go back. We, as human beings, go backwards if we are not going forward. So if we refuse to assume liability for our words and deeds, by continually blaming another for our own faults, then we, by default, slam it into reverse and leave a trail of blazing hell behind us.

Wading into the troubled waters of a blended family can cause great challenges. The current can be strong. The water can be icy cold. The rocks under your naked feet can slice through even the toughest calluses. The waves can easily push you over and the undertow can even pull you away. But there is always the safety net of the healthy blended family that keeps its members in tow. They wade into that water, whatever the condition, together. There is an attitude of teamwork and a sense of fair play. Love and respect, in a healthy blended family, is the name of the lifeboat they carry with them.

It is quite another thing, though, to be thrown into the raging sea with no lifeline at all. That is certain death. That is the toxic family. There is no escaping the deathly waters in this scenario. They do not forgive. They do not give in. They do not let up and they do not succumb. You need to build a bridge to safely cross these tumultuous seas.

> "A toxic person is someone who seeks to destroy you. A toxic person robs you of your self-esteem and dignity and poisons the essence of who you are. He or she wears down your resistance and thus can make you mentally or physically ill. Toxic people are not life-supporting. They see only negative in you. Jealous and envious, they are not happy to see you succeed. In fact, they get hostile whenever you do well. Their insecurities and feelings of inadequacy often cause them to sabotage your efforts to lead a happy and productive life."
>
> —LILLIAN GLASS, PHD (*Toxic People*)

Toxic people, however they manifest their toxicity, have issues of low self-esteem. If a person is self-absorbed with insecurity or even self-hatred, how can they possibly feel good about themselves or respond appropriately to anyone else in their lives? The toxic person has made themselves unavailable to respect or to love themselves and others. You might ask at this point, "How do I know if I am touched by a toxic person or relationship?" If I could sum up this complicated answer into one sentence, I would say that if a person in your life, in any capacity, uses their insecurities and feelings of inadequacy to deny you the offer of respect and dignity in any aspect of the relationship you hold with them, you have encountered a toxic relationship. And for your own sanity and health, it must be dealt with.

According to Dr. Lillian Glass, there are thirty types of toxic manifestations. If you even suspect that you are dealing with a toxic person in your family, past family, or in your life at some level, study her book! *Toxic People* is an absolute must-read. Dr. Glass hits the nail on the head and gives you, the should-be ex-victim, a fighting chance to break free, once and for all. To "unplug" is the term she gives to the breaking free process. She discusses ten techniques to handle toxic people and offers valuable information to choose the proper technique for the corresponding "toxic terror."

Dealing with toxic people is serious and dangerous territory. This area and its treatment must be left to the professionals in the field and I am not that. I believe that we can recognize toxic relationships that we might be involved in, but it takes professional advice to break free in the healthiest way for you and your family. Having stated that, I believe the key to freedom from a toxic person, relationship, or even a toxic memory, is forgiveness. Sometimes this word is ambiguous. But I think it is simply a two-bit word for "let it go." My phrase of choice, when I found myself in that position was, and still is, "Blow it off and get on with your life." It sounds glib and uncaring, but in actuality it took me ten years to blow it off, even though I carried on with my life quite quickly. You see, this toxicity not only involved me, but my children. I was like a mother bear protecting her cubs. So in order for complete and honest forgiveness to constantly run through my veins, I had to come to terms with a very complex toxic web of emotions and actions which affected the people I loved and cared for the most.

When faced with these types of troubles, we have the tendency to ask, "Why me?" And this is a natural question. Nonetheless, it is unanswerable if we want to break free and get on with our lives. I have always used this motto: "It is not what is on your plate, but how you are going to deal with it!" Life happens and we all encounter different challenges. The challenges will vary from person to person, but the important piece is how we handle the challenge. However, when there is no cooperation from the toxic person, it is necessary to break free altogether. Forgiveness is unequivocally the most important key to unlocking your complete freedom. And it all depends on you, not the tox-icity, however it rears its poisonous head.

> "When we understand the underlying reasons
> for people's actions, we can gain compassion
> and in turn forgive them."
> —Lillian Glass, PhD (*Toxic People*)

It is healthy and good for all people involved to make their final goodbyes to a toxic relationship, with love and not hatred in their hearts. If we are able to do this, we have overcome being a toxic victim. We have successfully eaten up our hatred for the relationship and its outcome and we have courageously fought back with the most powerful tool, which is love. In this case, love does conquer all.

> "The philosopher Nietzsche once said, 'That
> which does not destroy you makes you
> stronger.' How right he was! When you are
> able to handle the people in your life who
> make you miserable, you will definitely be-
> come a much stronger and more secure per-
> son. Your inner strength will allow risk taking
> in your career and in your social life, thereby
> creating a richer, fuller, and more adventurous
> journey through a life that is filled with posi-
> tive, good, and exciting things."
> —Lillian Glass, PhD (*Toxic People*)

As difficult and unappealing as this process might appear, it is extremely necessary for you personally. We would all take pleasure to forget our bad memories and just move forward, but our inner self will not allow this. The love in us, even for the people we have affection for, will be skewed. But it is this same power of love, in us, that will allow us to forgive the toxicity we have experienced in our lives. This in turn will set us free to love the people in our lives, unconditionally. And if we can believe this, it will allow us to love—maybe not actually like, but love—the toxic relationship that was necessary to unplug from in the first place. It is not that you must go back and have some sort of great relationship develop, but in your heart and soul you no longer experience the pain of victimization. And, at some point, when circumstances tolerate it, you might even be able to exchange a civil conversation. Now you are free to love, and laugh, and live.

The lowest ebb is the turn of the tide.

> *"When you cease to make a*
> *contribution, you begin to die."*
> ELEANOR ROOSEVELT

WINTER

"The bravest sight in the world is to see a
great man struggling against adversity."
SENECA

FOUR
GUARANTEED TO BLOW YOUR MIND

"You got your green eyes from your mother, and your freckles from your father. But where did you get your thrill-seeking personality and talent for singing? Did you learn these from your parents or was it predetermined by your genes? While it's clear that physical characteristics are hereditary, the genetic waters get a bit more murky when it comes to an individual's behaviour, intelligence, and personality. Ultimately, the old argument of nature vs. nurture has never really been won. But we do know that both play a part."
KIMBERLEY POWELL (*Nature vs. Nurture*)

Some scientists consider that we humans behave as we do in agreement with a genetic predisposition. This explains the "nature theory" of human behaviour. Still others think that we humans conduct ourselves in particular ways because we are taught to and we therefore become a product of our environment. This is known as the "nurture theory." Scientists will always keep this debate alive. Just how much we are shaped by our genetic make-up or how much we become a product of our environment remains to be seen. I figure that both come into play in a very prominent way.

But this is where, in a blended family, we encounter some challenges. It is especially taxing if some or all of the children share homes with both of their biological parents, which is usually the case. The children are expected to behave appropriately in each of their respective households. In a blended family, there are several, very different gene pools represented and there are many different environmental demands put on the children. No wonder we throw up our arms in absolute disbelief and great frustration when a member of the family does or says something that is valid and right in their eyes, but ridiculous and unacceptable in our own eyes. Now there's a recipe for utter chaos and dysfunction.

So who are we, anyway? We need to be sensitive to each member of the family, regardless of their genetic pool, predispositions, learned behaviour, or environmental attitude. Oh… is that *all*? It is a very *tall* order, indeed!

It is said that a child's personality and characteristics are formed by the time they are five years old. If there was great emotional, physical, or psychological damage done in these early years, there will be much work to be done in order to right some of these wrongs. But surely, not every wrong can be made right.

It is quite effortless to get a small child to do what you want him or her to do. Children plain out believe what their parents tell them. While this technique might save an adult time and energy, this is absurdly injurious to the psyche of the child. The adult takes full advantage of the innocent child's belief system and uses trickery to get what they want. It is as easy as swaying a child to a particular opinion by only explaining a one-sided school of thought. It demeans the value of a child and, in a worse way, eventually over time provides the child with the power to influence others in order to get what they want. This is a highly common method which promotes lying, cheating, and manipulation techniques. However, it is unethical, abusive, and a breach of confidence and trust with your child. Do we really want our children to be products of this type of environment? This sort of parental manoeuvring is obviously inappropriate and harvests caustic and even criminal behaviour in teens or young adults. The adult resorts to implementing guilt and requires a need-based love which both confuses and emotionally scars a child. Their mental facility is not developed enough to recognize such techniques, let alone understand how to cognitively deal with them. The adult's need for control is the unhealthy issue and needs to be addressed and overcome. But that would be subject to another book, and left to the professionals. Suffice it to say that this type of parenting is immature and devious. It helps no one involved.

As adults, we do not want to pass down to our children the troubles in our lives that we have been too cowardly to deal with for ourselves. As a parent, our goal should include acting as an excellent role model. It is important to display to your children that it is possible to overcome an issue and become a better person for it. We are all in this together… parent, stepparent, child, stepchild, and half-sibling alike. When it comes to personalities, parents, having the adult status, should not by default have the final authority in this arena. No matter what our age, we all fall short of perfection and every one of us needs to better ourselves in some way. Our world would be a better place if we would teach our children to deal with problems, issues, and undesired behaviours. But I suppose a prerequisite needed to win the privilege to fulfil this high calling would be that we, as adults, first of all try it out on ourselves!

Parenting is a great and awful responsibility. Our children are not our own to do with as we please. Children are a gift from God and God has graciously entrusted us with their care and holds us accountable to that awesome responsibility. Our job is to teach, instruct, and nurture our children, whatever their genetic coding. And we are responsible to provide a healthy and thriving environment for our kids to grow up in. There are basically two types of environments that we can offer our families. One is full of failure to live up to unattainable standards, therefore full of disappointment and constant condemnation. The other is simply full of grace. Grace is the atmosphere that covers all hurt. Grace is the environment that allows all new concepts to grow. If we are gracious to one another, each person will be nurtured and rise up into who they are meant to be. The definition of grace brings this into clarification. Grace is dignified, polite, and decent behaviour. Grace is the capacity to tolerate, accommodate, and forgive people. If it is a blossoming, blended family that we want, then developing and providing a surrounding of grace is indispensable. We are to prepare our children to become vigorous and hearty in spirit, soul, and body. Then they, in turn, can offer who they are and who they have become to their communities, their future families, and to our world at large.

So we have no excuses. All we are obligated to do is our very best for our children. They are, beyond doubt, worth the effort.

So the question still rages on… nature or nurture? I have purposed in my heart to do all that I can to nurture my family, and I leave to God what is God's.

FiVE

RATED X

Just what do you mean by that comment?" she sarcastically responds.

"What do you mean, what do I mean? It doesn't get any clearer than that," he angrily shouts back.

"Mom? Mommy, I want to watch my show now!" Kira whines as she pulls at her mother's shirt.

"Not now! Can't you see I'm busy?" she snaps back at her daughter. "You can go and tidy your room, right now."

"But you promised," she says to her mother.

"Do it now, Kira," her dad commands.

"Why?" Kira demands.

"Because I said so, that's why!"

In the new family dynamic, discipline must be the first and foremost mountain to climb. That mountain rests on the shoulders of the parents. However, it is the parents, in this new family, who need the strict discipline. Stepparent or biological parent, we must discipline ourselves to react and respond to each other and our children with respect and honour. We set the tone for the family.

> "Whenever adults are not actively working to identify and solve their own problems, then the focus on children may be especially intense or children may volunteer to deflect, detour and act our adult issues in most imaginative ways. Indeed, children tend to inherit whatever psychological business we choose not to attend to."
>
> Dr. Lerner (*Dance of Intimacy*)

It is certainly imperative to recognize and remember that it is our example that the children will follow. We are the teachers in the home and we need to be accountable to one another, as adults in the family setting. What we do is what our children will do. People learn by example and kids will hold you to that fact. If we do not "practise what we preach," the kids won't either. To take it even a step further, it is possible not to preach at all. If we are strict with ourselves and respond accordingly and in a united fashion, our actions will speak louder than our words.

This very issue reminds me of the *Peanuts* cartoon.

Did you notice that the words and voices of all the adults in this cartoon are jumbled and unintelligible? The children in the cartoon hear the parents in this way: *"Wha wha wha wha."* Ideally, our actions should be able to drown out the boring and monotonous words that are supposed to explain the desired behaviour.

> "The people who make the biggest impression on us are not those who tell us how to live, but those who show us how to live."
> —KAY ADKINS (*I'm Not Your Kid*)

The first and foremost task is setting the ground rules, but these particular household rules have nothing at all to do with the kids. These rules are for the parents. They must be well thought-out, discussed, agreed upon, and strictly instituted by the parents and the parents alone. There is nothing more destructive to a family than a situation where the children, who were initially being dealt with, witness an argument by the parents about their disagreement regarding the issue with the kid! Any smart kid will immediately glean, at that very instant, that dodging any responsibility for their actions is easy. All they need to do is get the two adults to disagree about the issue at hand. It is usually accomplished by an appeal to the heartstrings of the biological parent, in front of the stepparent. If, at that point, the parents have not unequivocally agreed and vowed to follow through with their plan of action concerning the children, the child will get off scot-free. The parents will have given in to the sidetracking scheme and enter into another, and unrelated, heated issue with each other. This scenario is counterproductive and destructive, but a highly common and repeated pattern that can occur in a blended family.

> "Self-control sometimes means putting aside
> your own preferences in order to maintain
> that powerful solidarity with your spouse."
> —KAY ADKINS (*I'm Not Your Kid*)

So how do we handle this crucial, yet delicate situation? I believe we, the adults, need to take our cues from the children. There is something to be said for approaching life and its problems as a child does. Their attitudes, trust levels, cavalier response to being incorrect, and need for power differs greatly from the adults' view of things. Recognizing and acknowledging this difference is most beneficial for true transformation and learning on the part of the adult. We adults have learned to outgrow this child-like vulnerability out of unfortunate necessity. As we grow older and mature, we realize that people can and will take advantage of us and over time we become calloused. Slowly, our thin and vulnerable skin hardens from the abuse and we wise up to this fact. Consequently, we shed our softer, innocent side for a life of watching our backs and ruthlessly controlling our circumstances and the people in our lives. Then, by our actions or unthinking words, we turn around and teach our children to do the same.

> "Whoever then humbles himself as this child, he is the greatest in the kingdom of heaven. And whoever receives one such child in My name, receives Me."
>
> —MATTHEW 18:4-5

I believe that vulnerability is an extremely powerful force. When we are vulnerable to others, we are transparent. Hence this freedom shows that we have nothing to hide. In this state, nothing inhibits us from true and pure relationship with others because we then become truthful and authentic. It is naked trust. It is how a child believes and sees the world. This is precisely why we need to protect them while nurturing them and modelling this behaviour. We, in turn, teach them that in this fragile state of vulnerability and transparency, there is great power and conviction. When we are truly genuine with our spouses and children, we can experience excellent communication and inherent respect for each other.

I believe it is from this basis that we need to establish the ground rules in our homes. Creating a mission statement for your family would both set a standard for acceptable behaviour and facilitate quality relationships among the members of the family unit. It is helpful to remember that we should not seek to control each other or situations that arise, but come together with a child-like belief to sort out our differences, and air our opinions and thoughts, so as to live in as much love and harmony as is possible. It is the responsibility of the adults to set the stage and keep themselves in check. Interestingly, the children, naturally, already got it goin' on. We need to nurture one another and never take that for granted. Let us uncloud and un-shroud the adult games of non-truth that we play, and allow the spirit of the children to run free in all of us.

ſix

IF AT FIRST YOU
DON'T SUCCEED...

"The dialogue with God which begins with the confession of one's own failures is not depressing; it is liberating. At last, perhaps even for the first time, we have been honest with ourselves about what we are; and we have been honest with the one Person before whom there is no deception."
EMILY GRIFFIN (*The Cup of Our Life: A Guide to Spiritual Growth*)

Failure is a huge and awful part of our lives. Our marriages have failed. Some relationships have failed. Our families have failed. We have failed our families. Failure is inevitable and sometimes unavoidable. We will fail. It is, indeed, a fact of life. However, we reactively respond to failure in very different ways. Some are beneficial responses and some are not. Many of us would finish this quote in varying ways.

If at first you don't succeed... blame someone else.

If at first you don't succeed... change the rules.

If at first you don't succeed... destroy any evidence that you even tried.

If at first you don't succeed... do it the way someone else does it.

If at first you don't succeed... make it someone else's problem.

If at first you don't succeed... lower your standards.

If at first you don't succeed... you probably never will.

If at first you don't succeed... quit.

These responses to the statement require absolutely no effort on our part. This is a lazy man's way. It accomplishes nothing. But if we are being truthful, we will admit that every one of us have either thought of or acted on one or more of these responses, at some time in our lives. Don't fret. We are all in this together. There is a more excellent way to handle this statement, however it does require a little more effort.

> "If at first you don't succeed... try, try again."
> —W. C. Fields

On the average, successful people have had many more failures than unsuccessful people. It is not the failures that they focused on. They concentrated on what to do after the failure. Successful people learn from their mistakes, changing their methods and trying the task again. This is the difference between successful people and unsuccessful people. This is the difference between successful marriages and unsuccessful marriages. This, too, is the difference between successful blended families and unsuccessful ones. We can be assured that the going will get tough. This is the time to dig in your heels and fight. As a side note, however, I must remind you that we should fight only for the proper and appropriate causes. Holding your ground and defending your own selfish desires, in spite of what is right, true and admirable, is an absolute disgrace and will surely lead you into much more trouble. Once you have determined the honourable cause, this is when your passion for your family should rise up, from deep within you, and your stick-to-itiveness should be on the frontline.

However, nobody ever said it would be fun or easy. This is where the rubber meets the road. This is where we find out what we are made of. This is where we find out what the other members of our family are made of. When the pressure is on, how *do* we respond? How *should* we respond? Simply put, we cannot quit. We have to try and try again. If one method does not solve the issue, then try another. If you experience one failure after another, console yourself in the fact that you are getting that much closer to being a success, with every failure that you experience. Stick to it. You owe it to yourself and to your family.

> "For what credit is there if, when you sin and are harshly treated, you endure it with patience? But if when you do what is right and suffer for it you patiently endure it, this finds favour with God."
>
> —1 PETER 2:20

Your hard work and efforts will pay off in the end. We need to practice the art of perseverance and daily soak in the thoughts of optimism. These two concepts must be at the forefront of our minds; first as thoughts, then as words, and finally as deeds. Our circumstances, situations, and family dynamics vary greatly, but the pathway to the blissful family will be paved, always, with persistence and optimism. Remember: it is the successful people who have failed more times than the unsuccessful people.

> "Those who wish to succeed must ask the right preliminary questions."
>
> —ARISTOTLE

These preliminary questions need to be elemental and appropriate to the unique set of circumstances that present themselves in your family. What are the pressing issues? What needs to be dealt with immediately, for safety or emotional health reasons? What issues need time to be worked out and are not beneficial to tackle at that moment? What are the requirements of your children, and are they being met? What can you do to meet those needs? What are your own needs, and are they being met? And most importantly, by who? It is essential to consciously and deliberately think about these questions and find, by whatever means available to you, the resources to handle the issues. I implore you to understand the importance of trying, and trying again. As tiring and exasperating as some situations and people can be, it is well worth your effort if it is a thriving and flourishing family that you are seeking to develop. It is helpful, especially in times of defeat, to remember these words...

If at first you don't succeed... try, try again.

SEVEN

!@%$#@

Who the "!@%$#@" do you think you are?

I am sure, if you are reading this book, that you would have had an occasion to fill in the bleeps with your own choice words. In a blended family, there are many different characters suddenly tossed into the mix. From the get-go, they are expected, for some odd reason, to get along. Some of us want things to go back to the ways things were. Others want to be in charge of everything, some want to keep the peace at all costs, while others do not want to be there at all. So the clashing and gnashing begins.

Anger can be a nasty thing, but it is a step that is necessary and should not be avoided. Most of us associate anger with negativity, but it has its advantages when expressed correctly. Anger is actually a meaningful expression of our deepest passions. Without anger, these ardent emotions might never surface. Anger will provoke your passions. And anger is provoked by love. We need to pay attention to it. Why are we so mad? What, in our deepest selves, is driving this passion to the surface? Why do we feel so strongly about an issue? That is your passion, your deepest wish. The answers to these questions will reveal your deepest passions and display your dreams and imaginings. Anger reminds us of what we really care about. We must stay aware of our anger. I do no think that directed anger is wrong. I believe it to be absolutely essential in certain instances.

Even Jesus got angry, but He handled his anger correctly. Great righteous indignation rose up from within Him as He lashed out against the Pharisees and the money changers in the temple.

> "They arrived at Jerusalem. Immediately on entering the Temple Jesus started throwing out everyone who had set up shop there, buying and selling. He kicked over the tables of the bankers and the stalls of the pigeon merchants. He didn't let anyone even carry a basket through the Temple. And then he taught them, quoting this text: 'My house was designated a house of prayer for the nations;

you've turned it into a hangout for thieves.'"

—MARK 11:15-17 (MSG)

Here Jesus had a solid reason to be angry and was compelled to right this wrong. He simply got angry and made a strong point. It is important to note, though, that He did not lash out against the people. He lashed out against their actions and explained why their behaviours were unacceptable. He revealed their heart attitude and taught them what was right. Even through the rage, His motivation was love. He was infuriated because He was moved with compassion and the deepest desire of His heart was revealed. He was incensed, but He did not sin. That is constructive anger.

There are two negative ways to fuel the fires of anger: rage and repression. Rage will harness the anger and lash out against anything or anyone that is available or blame-able at the time. This action does very little to productively channel this energy. It just hurts someone else. Repression is just as destructive, but is directed inwardly, to the angry person himself. He or she quietly swallows and stifles the negative energy. We have been trained to think this is the better of the two responses, because we can seemingly control the outbursts. But the pressure cooker can only hold so much steam before it explodes. The implosion happens within the person. It can manifest in all sorts of physical ailments or psychological sufferings. So neither response in healthy.

In the movie *Anger Management*, Jack Nicholson's character becomes absolutely and unjustifiably livid when his breakfast is not prepared to his liking. Even though this outburst was intentional at the time, we see this very commonplace anger reaction. Rage is a common expression for anger. In a different scene, Adam Sandler's character could not express anger at all. He allowed everyone in his life to walk all over him and this was destructive to all his relationships. These two characters displayed their anger in opposite ways. Both responses are inadequate.

However, there can be productive and constructive approaches to anger management. Resolution and redirection give us two examples of healthy responses to anger. Resolution is twofold. One must first acknowledge one's anger with a person or situation. Secondly, a commitment to working it out with the object of your anger is essential. If this can be done, it is demonstrated that the relationship is valued enough to confront and rectify the issues. But... it takes two to tango. Each party must be willing to engage in these necessary steps or you will continue to travel upstream with only one paddle. You will not get far without the cooperation of both parties. It is vital to remember that we, individually, take charge for our actions and how we choose to convey our anger. The outcome of this shared responsibility is deeper love and respect and care for one another.

Then again, sometimes the parties do not see eye to eye. In this case, redirection is the next best step. Redirection occurs as a result of two people disagreeing with each other about the methods to solve the anger issue. Like resolution, redirection is twofold. First, the parties need to demonstrate enough maturity to recognize that they can agree to disagree about a subject. Secondly, they can redirect their energies to a constructive force by positively investing this energy into someone else's life. There has never been a better remedy for calming yourself down than helping someone else. Advance this dynamic technique into another's life, and satisfaction will result. It is a great feeling and it works.

In these methods of accurately handling anger, there is one common thread that must be addressed. This is *love*. Love fuels the anger management practice. Should there not be enough devotion and esteem for the person in question, there will be no resolution. This is precisely why some conflict resolution situations never succeed. There are questions that beg to be answered.

1. Are you committed to this relationship in love and respect?
2. Do you care enough about the person and less about yourself to give it your full and dedi-

cated effort? This is the time to get real. Being true to yourself is a prerequisite to being true to another.

3. How do you really feel about the people in your blended family?
4. Are they worth your effort and enthusiasm?
5. Are you willing to sacrifice your own feelings, at times, for these people you live with?

Whatever your answers to these questions might be, you will know the truth, and depending on what you do with it, the truth will set you free.

SPRING

"And not only this, but we also exult in our
tribulations, knowing that tribulation brings
about perseverance; and perseverance,
proven character; and proven character,
hope; and hope does not disappoint, because
the love of God has been poured out within
our hearts through the Holy Spirit who was
given to us."

ROMANS 5:3-5

EiGHT

YOU SHALL KNOW
THE TRUTH

"But when the Friend comes, the Spirit of the Truth,
he will take you by the hand and guide you into all
the truth there is."
JOHN 16:13 (MSG)

I sat up on the kitchen counter, like a little kid, as my husband told me he did not love me anymore. In fact, he never loved me and he never wanted to be married and he never wanted kids. As he belaboured the point, thick with reasons and excuses, I saw him gesture, but I could no longer hear his voice. As his figure moved into slow motion, I slowly drifted into myself. Intuitively, I knew that inside me, somewhere was the strength I needed for that very moment. Running up the stairs to the privacy of my bedroom, I fought back the tears until I was alone. I quietly took my usual spot on the floor, propped up against the side of the bed, and stared out the window into the cloudless blue. The sky seemed empty and vacant. I could relate to its airiness and transparency. The truth is confronting. The truth is painful. It was the day that I somehow mustered the might and guts to choose to hear, to choose to understand, and to choose to know the truth.

> "And you shall know the truth, and the truth shall make you free."
>
> —JOHN 8:32

The scripture is accurate, but we can easily discount it. The truth can indeed set you free, but it is dependant on our treatment of the truth. The truth can also keep you bound. Once we know the truth, there is a glaring judgment staring us in the face, just imploring for a choice to be made. What will we do with the truth? If we embrace it and boldly alter our ways, our lives will transform and we will be free. If we hide from the truth, we keep ourselves chained and welcome more burden into the circumstances.

Through this telling experience of truth, I will never forget the terror I felt. My anguish and frustration and loathing seemed to mix into one sour and sickening drink that I actually dared to sip. Then I could feel the Spirit within me, rising to my consciousness, bringing the thoughts and intents of God from my subconscious mind to my conscious mind, that I would know the truth. It was an epiphany and marked the entrance to my freedom.

The truth came to me first of all because I truly wanted it to. But that was not always the case. I lived, for years, never glancing at it. I was too afraid, and fear is paralyzing. Fear is a trap that will keep us bound and enslaved. But truth, even though it can bring sorrow, pain and death, is the key to unlock all deception that so imprisons us. But I found out that the truth is gentle. It does not come smacking down on us all in one blow. The truth is served to us piece by piece. One truth leads to another and so fits in its place like a puzzle piece. Its unfolding is as tender and careful as the delicate wings of a butterfly unfolding for the first time. I believe it is so because truth comes from within, straight from the heart. To accept the truth, we choose to live from the inside out. To refuse the truth, we choose to die from the inside out. Herein lies the beauty of free will. We actually elect our own ways. Some paths look happier than others, but as I always say, "the grass is *not* greener on the other side of the fence." We choose to win or lose. We choose to accept or refuse. Sometimes, we need to search deep inside ourselves and listen to the still, small voice that is always vying for our attention. I think that inside all of us is the wisdom that we seek. We need to uncover it in ourselves, throw caution to the wind, and just believe.

As I sat on my bedroom floor, I opened a note I received from a very dear friend. It read,

> "You know God is with you no matter what door you walk through. His light and truth will lead the way."

In the midst of the turmoil of my life that day, I felt strong and filled with great confidence. But more than that, I had an overwhelming feeling of freedom. I was free from the fear that gripped me and, in turn, freed from myself and my preconceived ideas of my life, my marriage, and my family. The control was no longer mine. I was truly free. And as I stared out my bedroom window once again, the cloudless sky was clear and vivid and vast and limitless. And again, I could relate to the sky. I was clear and limited to nothing as well.

> *The Lord empties before He fills and He*
> *weakens before He strengthens; just the*
> *more deeply to impress that great truth, that*
> *success is not by might or by power, but by*
> *the Spirit of the Lord."*
> GINA'S JOURNAL # 5

NiNE

"NODA RUSHIN"

These are the most fondly and wisely spoken words that my Gramps repeatedly told me. From his thick Italian accent into his broken English, he would say, "Noda rushin." Translation: not a rushing—meaning don't rush; slow down. Even at the dinner table, he would half raise his voice, motioning to me, and say, "Heya you… whena you shew ona da food, you shew ita thirty-a-two times. That isa ahow youa diagesta yo food. Noda rushin. Whata ya gotta do, anyaway? What isa da bigga hurry? Alla wea gotta do isa eat! Come on. Havea a little avino… it helps ayou wita da food. Likea I sais, noda rushin!"

We live in an instant world. It really isn't instant, but we really want it to be and we try very hard to make it that way. We want what we want, when we want it, and that is usually… *now*! The blended family does not run smoothly this way. It takes time to blend. It requires the steady and paced order of every day and every moment in life. It is the slow and steady output of daily life that will produce the measured and stable results of family life. It is an incredible journey if we allow it to be.

Alcoholics Anonymous has a saying, "Let go and let God." I am aware of no superior way to begin and maintain the quest of a blended family than by forever staying true to this adage. It is vital to make a cognisant resolution to slow down. It does not come naturally to us, though. It requires constant allegiance to sustain this type of mindset in our hectic world. Moreover, it is urgent in a blended family because there are such numerous values and ideas within the nucleus that tempers can escalate with little prompting. If we do not settle to let cooler heads prevail, resentment and anger can make their home with us. This could be the beginning of the end. But this entire process takes time. I find it helps to write down a few guidelines, so I have a safeguard that allows me to refer back to my strategies and keep myself and my family in check when I am struggling and my mind races beyond reason.

When a situation arises and there is need for restoration of order, refer to these simple but effective strategies to get you back on track.

"Noda Rushin"

Identify the Problem

One member of the family will present a problem in a utterly different way than another member of the family. We do this because we want the outcome of the issue to lie in our favour. But we must, first of all, spot the root of the issue. We need to get to the truth of the matter.

Let Go … and Let God

This is one of the most difficult things to do, but it is the one thing that will bring complete restoration to a situation. If each party drops their argument, there comes a straightforwardness in finding a solution. The wrongs will be identified and solutions can be established and initiated.

Right at that moment, take some time to have some fun with each other. Take some time to display your love and respect for each other. It could be as simple as a tickling session or a card game or planning an outing. In these times, actions can speak louder than words.

I thinks Gramps was right. Take the time to love each other and work it out. Sweeten up your life and relationships by making great family time together. Make it count and respect all involved. In the scope of life, a few moments together as a family will add years of happiness.

Ignorance is not bliss. Deal with the matters at hand.

"What isa da bigga hurry?"

TEN

SO YOU WANT
A DREAM HOME

*"In reaching for guidance about our dreams, we are
reaching toward God. Our dreams are not futile.
They do not spring from our egos. They have their
roots in our souls."*
JULIA CAMERON (*Finding Water*)

Then dream on!

When you want to build your dream home, you have to first start dreaming. Where do you buy the piece of land? What area would be suitable for your family in relation to school and work locations? Do you want a bungalow or a multi-level home?

Then you need to dream about the plan of the house. Usually we research this with a builder and we can take a look at plans for different homes. We can tweak the plans to suit our needs and change the shape of certain rooms.

The sky is the limit when it comes to the options we have. So we dream about what we want in a house and how we want it to look.

Then we start thinking about the landscaping of the yard and where we want certain trees, shrubs, and flowers. As we make decisions and physically see the formal plans drawn on paper, we have no trouble believing that it will actually come to pass. We know that at some point this dream home and gorgeous yard will take form, on the plot of land that we purchased for it.

I like to think about the blended family life in the same way. We live in a time where even the traditional family does not work well, so how can we expect a blended family to be functional? If we can dream about it, and draw it out on paper, like the physical dream home, the blended family can be fleshed out and take on real form and be equally efficient. To achieve the goal of a successful and significant blended family life, it will take just as much and more dreaming, planning, buying, tweaking, working, and sweating than to construct that physical house. However, in building a blended family, you are building a home. If you think it is difficult to work with builders and tradespeople, just ponder for a moment the tireless effort and energy needed to build a blended home. At least the builders leave at the end of the day. In the blended family, the members stay 24/7. The work is never done. There is always something to fix or refine. While everyone is still living at home and dependant on each other, you are always in building mode. Yes… I concur that it does sound a little daunting, although I do not know of one great thing that was accomplished without an uphill, upstream challenge. Take heart; at least we're on the up and up.

If you keep the dream before you, you will not faint or get weary. On the contrary, you will be fully energized by the task and encouraged by the results of your careful and diligent work and dedication. So builders, dream on!

> "And then God answered: 'Write this. Write what you see. Write it out in big block letters so that it can be read on the run. This vision-message is a witness pointing to what's coming. It aches for the coming—it can hardly wait! And it doesn't lie. If it seems slow in coming, wait. It's on its way. It will come right on time.'"
>
> —HABAKKUK 2:2-3 (MSG)

> "There is a power within us that can go way beyond what we can think or imagine. Hold tenaciously to your dream."
>
> —TOMMY BARNETT (*Adventure Yourself*)

This is the stuff that dreams are made of.

Do you remember Jiminy Cricket, from Walt Disney's

'Pinocchio'?

> "When you wish upon a star,
> makes no difference who you are.
> Anything your heart desires
> will come to you.
> If our heart is in your dream,
> no request is too extreme.
> When you wish upon a star,
> like dreamers do.
> Fate is kind.
> She brings to those who love
> The sweet fulfillment
> of their secret longing.
> Like a bolt out of the blue,
> fate comes in and pulls you through.
> When you wish upon a star,
> your dreams come true."

This little Disney character sang this song and it was instantly famous, because it was true. The method he sings about might be fantastical, but the truth of the words, when executed by faith and true belief, can manifest your deepest desires. They can be brought from the subconscious, to the conscious mind and finally to the visible world we live in. If you allow yourself to dream and never let your dream go, the dream will come to you.

Be careful, however! It is extremely important to mention here that the dream you hold fast to may not manifest in exactly the same manner as you think it should or as you so sincerely desire it to. Do you remember as a child when your parents withheld something from you that you really wanted and they said it was for your own good? Then later in life, as your pondered that memory, you realized the wisdom in your parent's ruling. At the time, though, you were too young to understand the implications of the choice. What might transpire in your life, however, is the perfect manifestation of the exact answer to the problem. It is significant to bear in mind that the means to the end might be clothed in something different, greater, or better than we could even think or imagine. We do not want to miss the forest for the trees, do we?

As I mentioned before, the process of growing up into adults helps us lose our powerful and useful child-like ways. Maybe we should not grow up so fully.

Do you have any dreams, or do you just live from day to boring day? Stop for a moment and dream about your wishes for your blended family. What dreams do your children have? What do they want to glean from the whole family experience? When your kids are grown and gone away from the home, will you be satisfied with the family model you provided for them? Will they be fulfilled with the family model you provided for them? Did y'all have fun? Was it worth the trouble and heartache? Do not allow your family life to simply pass you by. You have to live every single moment of life, so you might as well enjoy and have fun, be productive, be educational, laugh, and experience rich family values. We need to think positively and encourage and spur one another on to dream and dream big. A great way to get everyone involved in this exercise is to form a Dream Team. Think up scenarios for the perfect life together, and then do it! Everyone can participate and it will encourage a sense of ownership and belonging.

Simply toss out a question like…

What do we want from family life?

What would make us happy?

What would make us sad?

What would make us laugh?

What activities do we like to do?

What kind of vacations do we want to take?

How does the dream family get their chores done?

What is the greatest thing that we could do as a family that we would be proud of?

Be sure to remember the answers to these questions, because those answers will dictate to you what you spend your life fighting for. You might want to write them down in big, bold letters so that everyone passing by can easily read them, on the run. Implement your ideas. Whatever you dream up, everyone will have taken part in the dreaming process and will look forward to working together to make it all come to pass. Every member will own the dream and will take pride in it. The key to your future lies in your dreams and your passions. Dream your dreams, and see your visions. Write them on tablets of stone. Keep them close to your heart and never let them go.

> "For the vision is yet for an appointed time and it hastens to the end [fulfilment]; it will not deceive or disappoint. Though it tarry, wait [earnestly] for it, because it will surely come; it will not be behindhand on its appointed day."
>
> —HABAKKUK 2:3 (AMP)

So who are you then? What has God made you to be? What is the blueprint for your life? Only your dreams can unlock the answers to these questions. Only your released passion can bring about the fulfillment of these dreams. Only the process of the journey can make the dreams a reality.

So dream on!

And live on!

And be who you were created to be!

SUMMER

"There is an appointed time for everything.
And there is a time for every purpose
under heaven."
<small>ECCLESIASTES 3:1</small>

ELEVEN

WRITE YOUR OWN STORY

At this point in the book, we are taking a breather. It is time to stop. It is time to listen. It is time to dream. Then, finally, it is time to obey your heart and purpose to do the things that it cries out for you to do.

Summertime for me is a time of adventure and revelation. I do my very best thinking and creating in this time of the year. It may be due to the fact that I immerse myself in nature and it gives back to me. I believe this is a strong and deliberate way in which God speaks to our hearts and gives us glimpses of things to come.

One summer, many years ago, I had a life-changing and most remarkable experience on the lake. It was not supernatural in a worldly sense, though it moved my spirit nonetheless. It was a simple occasion that made a lasting impact on my life. It gave me an image of something I wished my life would stand for. This understanding lives with me still. I suppose this is why I have written out my story. It inspires and encourages me to keep on keeping on.

Everyone should have a story that depicts the kinds of feelings and atmosphere that remind them of their desired family dynamic. It is crucial to get a mental picture of what you really want and to recall it often. Everyone's story is diverse and everyone's story is significant. Yours is uniquely and intensely personal and should, for you, bring you hope and courage to carry on. It is time to reflect and keep your story in mind. It is time to recount all the goodness and beauty and truth that your story needs to tell.

My story invokes relaxed and peaceful kinds of feelings that I want for my family situation. Its setting is a place where my family loves to be. This story helps me press on in my quest for a successful and noteworthy blended family, until it actualizes in my family life.

LAKE LIFE—MY STORY

The offshore breeze tosses hair in my face and the sands twist and sweep under my feet as I head for the lake. I heave my windsurfer flat on the water. The familiar slapping sound resonates in the bay. Climbing on my board, I smile, as if I was appreciating the wonder of the lake for the very first time. The sail flutters and dances until a gusty wind catches it and pulls us away. Cool water streams through my toes and over my feet as the board dips and rises with increasing speed. The beauty beckons us while the breath of the wind sets the pace. The trees on the shoreline look to be laughing as they lean in the warm summer breeze. The sharp smell of fish lingers where the blue herons pursue the constant hunt.

The distant hum of a motorboat speedily approaching the bay whizzes by me. Its rough wake sends my board into a frenzy of jumps. The shock of each wave smacks the bottom of my board as I pull hard on the bar. As I draw back to the water, my shoulder gets sprinkled. The sudden coolness sends shivers down my spine, but the sun warms and dries me with every hot surge of passing air. The haunting call of the common loon attracts my attention to the cove at the end of the island, where her young must be. Looking intensely, I drift close as the Mother Loon extends her body straight up and runs along the surface of the water, warning me with loud honking and squawking. Plunging under, she vanishes. I relax my grip as my sail luffs in the wind, and I let it quietly drop sideways, settling on the water. Kneeling, I am refreshed as the water laps my legs. The loon somehow senses my distance is safe, and she resurfaces, only this time closer to her nest. I search the shore, but her secret remains hidden. She is too clever for me.

The noonday sun beats down on my already scorched back as I lie down. I spy on the waves as they roll over me in playful splashes. I am so near nature, I can smell it. The dry scent of sand on the beach, the clean, fresh aroma of the waves all around me, and the air that strokes the lake trails the tangy whiff of fish. I am quite removed from the bustle of the beach. Out here, I am one with nature. I hear my heart beating in perfect time to the rippling surf, the swaying evergreens, and the fluttering flap of seagulls' wings. I can freely hear the symphony of creation.

Clearly echoing in the bay, our dinner bell sounds. I know it rings for me. So I make one last hurried surf straight to shore.

I often recount this story with the sense memory it brings back to me. I wrote it in a descriptive way, because I am a tactile person. I think in pictures and I need to be reminded that everything around me is precious. Every moment of every day offers me the opportunity to respond, and respond well. I also recall the feeling of such peace that day. I want to live there.

It is easy to live in harmony when we live in solitude and control and are free and able to just enjoy the beauty around us. Living in a blended family does not naturally enable this peaceful life. On the contrary, it is easy to encounter problems and issues and conflicts with people. But we always have a choice, and in the power of that choice lies the keys to our responses, and ultimately to our outcomes. Our stories help us to remember the kind of life we want to lead and this, in turn, helps us to make a choice that will eventually bring us closer to a place of peace in our lives. I remember that amidst all the things that I might face in my life, whether I am sure of them or not, I will make it through because it is my faith and my family that have given me a sense of sanctuary and well-being.

The toil and sweat that we pour into the lives of the people we love will unquestionably pay off. You get out of life what you put into it.

As you write your own story, make it real and believable and true. Allow its message to impact you and remind you of the vision you have for your life. Let its mood set yours and compel you to carry on. Let its setting be memorable and comfy and safe, because how we think of ourselves, that's how we will be.

TWELVE
STEP IT UP

Facts are facts, and some are cold and hard. In a stepfamily, one parent has no blood connection with at least one child. Therefore, this child belongs to one parent only. This child was created with someone that does not share in this home. This child then is under the authority and responsibility of a stepparent. This emotionally unnatural state, facilitated by separation, causes the child to lose their sense of belonging... in any home.

Incidentally, the same is true for a stepparent. When a sense of "unbelonging" sets in, we have a tendency to push our weight around in order to fit in. Do you remember when your toddlers would play with differently shaped blocks that fit into correspondingly shaped holes? With some time, they managed to get the square shape into the square shaped hole ,but if they struggled too much and got frustrated, what happened? They got angry. So next time, we stepped in to help them connect the shapes and they were satisfied, happy and proud of themselves.

It is similar in a stepfamily. If we do not have help to fit into the family setting and feel a sense of belonging, it is frustrating. But more than that, the members of the family feel out of place and uncomfortable. At this point, we need to step in and proactively facilitate an atmosphere of be-longing. We need to foster belongingness among all the members of the stepfamily.

Even if both primary and secondary households are relatively healthy, both the children and the parents living in these families need to feel that they belong there. It is common that the parents, either step or biological, want to rule the roost. And they should, to a certain extent. How-ever, there needs to be a respectful consideration for the feelings of the children, whether or not they preside with the family on a full-time or part-time basis. This task can be daunting. It introduces a whole new set of dynamics to the new family.

The "in-home" parent and the children have a specific and established method related to the decisions and go-ings-on in the family, while the stepparent, not to mention any other children that they bring into the mix, has an en-tirely different method to their own decision-making process. Then there is the weight of the ex-spouse of each of the in-home parents. And do not think for one moment that the children are not quick enough to know exactly what their other parent would say or do in any given situation. And they would naturally and happily use it against the in-home parents in order to gain some control over their situation.

Even though this behaviour is unacceptable, it is quite understandable, from the child's perspective. This picture I have just painted gives us just a glimpse of all the diverse and wide-ranging personalities, characters, ideas, opinions, methods, and general ways of life that can arise in the step-family.

So what can be done about all of this? Everyone, whether their designation is step, biological, half-, part-time, full-time, temporary, or permanent, has a deep need to belong. They must feel confident that this is their home and their family and that they are as much a part of it as anyone else. Their voices must be heard, their actions acknowledged, their successes praised, and their boundaries in place. They need to be loved and feel loved. They need to be safe and feel safe. They need to fully belong to the family.

I have found three main attitudes which influence and solidify this sense of belonging: Acceptance... Respect... Laughter.

It is a popular belief that if you accept yourself, you will be able to accept others more easily. In this context, however, I think the opposite is true. Accepting others, just as they are, is the key to being able to accept yourself. Always getting just what you want does not make for a happy home. Putting others first and serving them is the key to happiness and joy in a family. But I do understand fully that this reaction is not one that comes naturally. We need to find new ways to do new things with the new people in our blended lives. A good starting point is to find out what the people you live with like and dislike. Ask what makes them tick, or what makes happy or sad. Accepting people for who they are at that moment in life is a tremendously strong starting point and will instil a real sense of belonging. Communication is key to developing an acceptance type of relationship. Talk it up!

Respect is one of the most important aspects in a healthy family life. You may find varying philosophies, ideas, values, or opinions, but it is important to use these opportunities to practice your selfless acceptance and esteem, even in the face of disagreement or difference. Ask questions to determine their dreams, wishes, and aspirations. Then build on these together. Formulate a code of ethics that you all agree to follow. With this type of checkpoint in place, respect will flow more easily. When an issue arises, the set standards will help to solve the conflict to resolution. We will enable one another by facilitating each other to live by the methods we have collectively set out.

> "By working to resolve conflicts in our step-families, we demonstrate our desire for each person to belong and feel accepted and to know the fullness of the human experience."
> —KAY ADKINS (*I'm Not Your Kid*)

Laughter is a big deal. If the process of blending a family is not amusing and enjoyable, no one will want to participate. We first of all need to be able to laugh at ourselves. We will all make blunders. That is a certainty. Yet a defensive response only adds to the tension. We have to be tension breakers. Anyone who is excluded form the circle of love will someday have the ability to hurt you. In order to be happy, we need to learn to love imperfection. I do not mean to tolerate imperfection, but to actually love it. Not everything will work out in the way that we think it should. We need to laugh if off. It is important sometimes, and particularly in times of strain and stress, to take life a little less seriously. It is easy to get caught up in a matter, especially when it is close to our hearts. At that point, though, it would benefit you to remember my favourite quote: "And this too, shall pass." In the scope of life, is the concern so dire that a touch of humour can't lighten it a little? Use laughter to sweeten the blow and concentrate your efforts on finding a solution. When you choose to live in step with others, there will be countless opportunities to search for and find the good in each other's personalities. Meticulously work to incorporate the intrinsic worth of each member of the family. Encourage everyone to contribute to the whole. Harping on, complaining, and highlighting negative qualities only cause the family to fall out of step. Concentrating on positive characteristics and energies poises the family to live in step.

> *"I shall pass through this world but once.*
> *Any good therefore that I can do, or any*
> *kindness that I can show to any human be-*
> *ing, let me do it now. Let me not defer or ne-*
> *glect it, for I shall not pass this way again."*
> ANONYMOUS

THiRTEEN
TRUST THE DRIVER

*"If you trust absolutely, you will always be receptive
enough to the signals that life and God and yourself—your deep self—will be giving you. You will always be given the clue, the information, and the inspi-
ration to carry you through."*
ANDREW HARVEY (*The Cup of Our Life*)

I t is Sunday early in the day, early in the week, and
early in the spring. The cars are not racing past the
house today. No one is in a hurry to get anywhere.
There is a dabbling of traffic, but mostly the streets are
bare. Only a few cars pass by. Peering out my studio window, I search for my thoughts. It is quiet and still, except
for the rare sighting of the Bohemian Waxwing. They are
all aflutter in the trees, feasting on the frozen berries.
These birds are an irregular winter visitor from the far
north, if the supply of fruit on the trees is scarce. Their
coats are colourful and vibrant. Their dance is directed

and purposeful, but wild and free. It is extremely uncommon to see them this far from their natural habitat. I guess they are hungry and God has drawn them here, where the berries are. I wonder, would God, who simply directs the birds, possibly direct me to a place where I will be nurtured and happy? I believe He would!

> "For this reason I say to you, do not be worried about your life, as to what you will eat or what you will drink; nor for your body, as to what you will put on. Is not life more than food, and the body more than clothing? Look at the birds of the air, that they do not sow, nor reap nor gather into barns, and yet your heavenly Father feeds them. Are you not worth much more than they?"
>
> — MATTHEW 6:25-26

I realized that day that my life was not my own, and I was settled with that reality. It is important for me to live a life that is purposeful and directed. Because I do not know what lies ahead or what is to come, how then can I be certain that the decisions I make regarding my life are the correct ones? That is not to say that I glibly stumble through life hoping that good things will transpire just because. God forbid! But I can prayerfully choose my way, commit that way to the Lord, and do what I have purposed in my heart to do.

Let me illustrate this point. Have you ever tried to steer a car that is not moving? Having owned a few "beaters" in my life, I am all too closely aware of how impossible this task is. If the vehicle is not in motion, it is impossible to steer. The same truth applies to the principle of trust. If we are not in motion, by some act of our will, how can we trust that the Lord can direct our paths? In a stationary state, He simply cannot! However, once we are moving, even in the wrong direction, if we trust that He can direct our paths, He has the ability to change our course and steer our way. This is trust. It is not complicated, but we must be willing to move. We willingly take ourselves out of the driver's seat and go along for the ride.

When we know our purpose in a blended family, the meaning of our place in it becomes clear. When our purpose is meaningful, we can bear anything. Without a sense of function and position in the blended family, our hopelessness will prevail. Hope is the catalyst to carry us through any moment or event or happening. When you find your purpose in your blended family, what you need to accomplish becomes clear. The task might not be easy and may very well toss you out of your comfort zone, but at least, you *know* what you are to do. That is half the battle. The other half is executing the plan. This is where the rubber meets the road. Following through with a task is a difficult thing. It will stretch you in ways you might not want to be stretched, or even in ways that you might have thought were not even possible. It is precisely at this point that our reason must be clear. I believe that each and every one of us, with all our limitations, talents, quirks, and differences, was created with a very exact and distinctive purpose in mind.

I do not believe in chance. I believe in perfect design. Every one person is called to something outstandingly their own and in their own special way. No person can do what I am precisely called to do, except me. No one can do what you are specifically called to do, except you. If even the flowers of the fields in all the world are clothed in color and design very expressly, exceptionally and directly, would not each and individual person be called to something explicitly matchless and intended for them personally? I believe so! This purpose will pull us through the difficult times and drive us ahead into better weather. After all, we do it for our families. It is part of the undoing and redoing and rebuilding process of the blended family. The sacrifices and concessions we make for the good of our family ultimately gratify our own hearts. I always think of the old story about meeting St. Peter, at the gates of Heaven.

So this woman dies and she finds herself at the Pearly Gates. St. Pete says to her, "If you can spell

PURPOSEFUL, you can get into heaven." So the woman spells the word correctly and she makes it in. It is time for St. Pete's coffee break, so he asks this new woman to watch the Gates while he is gone. She says, "Well, what am I to do if someone comes?"

He replies, "Oh, that's easy. Just ask them the same question I asked you and if they answer incorrectly, have them stand on the left side of the gate. If they spell the word correctly, let them in ."

Meanwhile back on earth, her husband was so distraught at his wife's death that he, too, dies. All of a sudden, she sees her husband at the Gates. He is so happy to see her that he says, "Honey, we made it. I missed you so much."

As he moves in for a kiss, she holds up her hand and motions him back. "Hold on there, buster. You're not in yet. You have to answer one question. Are you ready? " she asks.

He thinks to himself, *If she can do it, I can do it, too.* He states, "Yes, I am ready." His wife stands upright and proudly says, "Spell Czechoslovakia."

Even though this is a silly little, joke there is great purpose in my telling it. We will one day find ourselves at the foot of God and He will ask us what we have done with the talents and gifts and energy and resources and children and family that He has given us. What will we tell Him?

What will we say to God? How will we answer the almighty Creator of the universe? Personally, I want to say that I purposed in my heart to do all that He created me to do and that I did all I could humanly do, in His power, to relay that very purpose to my children and my family. No matter how you spell it out, you must have an appropriate answer.

> "This is the true joy of life: the being used up for a purpose recognized by yourself as a mighty one; being a force of nature instead of a feverish, selfish little clot of ailments and grievances, complaining that the world will not devote itself to making you happy."
>
> —GEORGE BERNARD SHAW

> "Trust in the Lord with all your heart and do not lean on your own understanding. In all your ways acknowledge Him, and He will make your paths straight."
>
> —PROVERBS 3:5-6

FOURTEEN
TRUE CONFESSIONS

*"No individual has any right to come into this world
and go out of it without leaving behind him distinct
and legitimate reasons for having passed through it."*
GEORGE WASHINGTON CARVER

Hiding behind the adults' legs, timidly peeking around to snatch inquiring glances at me, she ventures forward with one tiny step. Now I am completely and utterly engaged in this child's play. I have intentionally overlooked and forgotten the conversation I was in. I spy, with my little eye, directed looks and glances, in order to edge the child forward. And this little two-year-old is oh so cute! She not only notices my interest, but she is now fully connected in our unspoken game. Her eyes are wide with curiosity and her body loosens with trust. We play a quick peek-a-boo and she emerges from her hiding spot.

I carefully crouch down to my knees and say, "Hello."

She stares back at me in what seems like desperate need and squeaks,

"Hi."

As I carefully reach into my pocket, her eyes follow my every move. Her anticipation rises as I slow down all my actions. She anxiously waits to see what I might pull out of my pocket. I advance, producing a wrapped candy, which I hold right in front of her face.

I say, "Do you like candy?"

She nods her head up and down.

I ask, "Do you think you would like this candy?" She stares up at her dad and quickly back to me.

She emphatically says, in a matter-of-fact way, "Yes, please!"

This simple interaction marked the beginning of a tried and true relationship with my stepdaughter.

Now I have the distinct pleasure of introducing you to the one whom I have known for twenty-six years. Since she is grown and has a family of her own, I felt it was important to include an excerpt from my stepdaughter's experience in our blended family. She writes:

"I was an only child until I was eight years old and moving back and forth between my divorced parents, when I was told that my stepmother was going to have a baby. My mind raced with the possibilities of just what it would be like to be a big sister! I was ecstatic, yet in my growing excitement there was a dark cloud threatening my ray of sunshine. I was distressed that I would only be with the new baby a day or two a week and every second weekend. This schedule did not seem like quite enough. And it would not have been. Even at the age of eight, I understood that I needed to be there in order to belong. I desired a true sense of family and this new little life was offering that very hope.

Within two years, I realized that I had the courage to start my life fresh and attempt to leave behind the disappointments in my life with my biological mother. I moved in full-time with my father, stepmother, and sister. At ten years old, I adapted to being part of a new family, while I licked the wounds over the collapse of my previous one. It was not as easy as simply wanting to be a part of my sister's daily life. I had to learn that toddlers end up trumping ten-year-olds for attention and that fathers can still be absent no matter how much more time you get to spend with them. I also learned that a stepmother can actually be a true mother. I learned that love can be given with no strings attached and that comfort and stability may be found from the person you least expect. My entire being was crying out for acceptance in this new family. What I did not imagine was to get it from the one person who truly owed me nothing. I found that there was no rhyme nor reason to love, so why do we automatically think that the bond of blood must tie us to each other?

In the coming years, our family morphed into different versions of its previous self. We added a bother, lost a father, added a stepfather, and another brother. Our family continues to change daily. The important thing is that we all remain true to each other despite the many twists and turns and roadblocks life can throw our way. Family is defined as a social unit living together. My family is more than that. We do not all live together anymore, yet our family grows stronger every year. It is our love that binds us. Not our blood. It is our diversity that keeps things interesting.

It is our mother that keeps us all together in the end. She has always said, "Amidst great adversity there is blossoming possibility." Our family has been tested over and over again and we have fought in the trenches of adversity. And here we are, with hands clasped tightly, staring straight toward the future, with the possibilities it holds for us, as a family.

Thank you, Mom... for never giving up and for always believing in the greatness of those you love. Thank you for striving for the unity of our family, and most of all, thank you for giving me my home. For being my home. I love you!"

The sun had set by the time we reached the old nunnery, a renovated and remodelled restaurant. It was our first real date after many long and stimulating conversations, casual social gatherings, and a little flirting. The brisk evening air snapped at my body as I stepped out of the car. But he was there to guide me to the path. As we walked side by side, without a word, he tenderly yet casually slipped his hand into mine. Then I realized it was not the evening air that snapped at my body. It was as if we fit into each other's rhythms and our connection shaped each passing moment we shared. Somehow I felt I finally fit into this world. I was comfortable and secure and sure of myself and my calling. I remembered, as a young girl, my desire for God and to live a life serving Him.

We arrived at the great wooden doors of the nunnery and I laughed to myself. I was found dawning the doors of a nunnery, holding the hand of the man that God had brought to me, so I could live that life serving God. My heart jumped within me and somehow we both knew that this simple gesture was the beginning of a new and beautiful symphony between us. As the evening wore on, I understood fully that the prayers, hopes, and dreams of a life once lived had culminated in this man that walked beside me. I was certain then that there was a blueprint for our lives and the life of our blended family.

We married a year and half later. Since he has a son of his own and is stepfather to my children and stepchildren, I felt it was important to include an excerpt from my husband's experience in our blended family. He writes:

"With all the challenges that a blended family poses, our reserves are tapped very quickly. Blending a family will work much more easily and efficiently if spiritual compatibility and cohesiveness is present. As we all draw closer to God, the super abundant peace flows. The seemingly impossible becomes possible. As you look into the eyes of your family, you know something wonderful is taking place. It is a work in progress, but it is taking place supernaturally. You realize that all the messy, blended family business was supposed to occur at a particular point in time. Gently, and sometimes not so gently, all our life experiences prepared us for what is laid before us. And as difficult and painful as some experiences are, I believe that it is well worth it in the end. If I, as a father and stepfather, can contribute something valuable and meaningful and lasting in any of my family members' lives, I will have accomplished something great."

Having read these true accounts of real people living

in a blended family, you can easily glean that it has all been well worth the heartache, and through it all, my blessings have been great.

Wind-Up and Wishes

"Now is not the end. It is not even the beginning of the end. But it is, perhaps, the end of the beginning."
Sir Winston Churchill
(November 1942)

As long as there is life and we still have breath, there is time. At any crossroad, no matter where we find ourselves and in whatever status, there is no time like the present to take up the cause and fight for our families. "Carpe diem," as they say. While we can, we must seize the day and make the most of every opportunity granted to us. We just have to start somewhere. And if we take a step back for a moment to really look at our present situations, evaluate where we are, and where we want to be, a simple starting point will dawn on us. Again, we just have to start *somewhere*.

I believe there is hope for everyone, for every situation and a solution to every problem. But that does not mean that we, personally and singlehandedly, have to come up with all the brilliant answers to these intricate troubles. We are not islands to ourselves. We desperately need each other, and please be assured that there is no shame in this. On the contrary, there is power in numbers and muscle in togetherness. There is a wealth of knowledge and understanding that we collect from each other and our experiences. Should we not tap into all of our resources in order to accomplish our goals, dreams, and aspirations for our families? To that I boldly declare, "Yes!" Yes, we should hold each other up and sustain our common cause for the family. It is our distinct privilege and duty to our families, our stepfamilies, our extended families, our communities, and our world.

And I sincerely wish good things for you and your family. I wish that your existence would be the best it can be. So in that vein, for you and yours, I paraphrase the following quote…

"If you listen to the voice of God and happily

obey His words, promptings and instructions, He will place you in a high position. All these blessings will rain down on you and beyond you, because you have answered His call for your life.

God bless you in the city,

God bless you in the country,

God bless your children, your stepchildren, and your half-children.

God bless your vocation and life's work, all of your belongings and possessions, all of your holdings and your livelihood.

God bless your goings and your comings and all that you set your hands to do.

God will defeat your enemies.

God will declare blessings on you and your spouse and all of your children.

God will bless the lands and the families that He has entrusted to you.

If you poise yourself and your family, just as He promised, God will make you holy and established. Don't swerve even an inch to the left or the right, but follow the still, small Voice of God that is inside you, and you and yours will be blessed of the Lord."

—DEUTERONOMY 28:1-14

It has been said, "Where there is a will, there is a way." We have been given free will so we have the liberty to choose our own way. The outcomes of our lives will directly result from the choices we have made. Much like gravity, this is a principle that does not change. It cannot be altered or even ignored. Whether we like it or not, our lives will lie in its wake. We have the power to choose our way and the proceedings will unfold. On the one hand there is life, and on the other there is death. On the one side there is light, and on the other darkness. All we have to do is choose and be willing to follow the signs on the road we have preferred. It has been my experience, both sorrowful and painful, yet joyous and satisfying, that a way has been paved for me where there seemed to be no way. In staying true to my choice, I found a spring in the middle of a desert. That is the work of God in my life and in the life of my blended family. So I carefully give credit where credit is due. Such high and honoured glory goes only and directly to God!

*Start by doing what's necessary; then
do what's possible; and suddenly you
are doing the impossible."*
ST. FRANCIS OF ASSISI

BIBLIOGRAPHY

Author unknown. *Humpty Dumpty*, nursery rhyme in the Mother Goose Collection.

President Lyndon B. Johnson's Commencement Address at Howard University: *"To Fulfill These Rights."* - June, 1965.

Glass, Lillian. *Toxic People: 10 Ways of dealing with people who make your life miserable*. New York: St. Martin's Press,1997.

Powell, Kimberly. *Nature vs. Nurture: Are we really born that way?* http.//geneology.about.com

Lerner, Harriet. *The Dance of Intimacy: A woman's guide to courageous acts of change in key relationships*. New York: Harper & Row, 1989.

Adkins, Kay. *I'm Not Your Kid: A Christian's Guide to a*

Healthy Step-family. Michigan: Baker Books, 2004.

Cameron, Julia. *The Sound of Paper: Starting from Scratch*. New York: Penguin Group, 2004.

Cameron, Julia. *Finding Water: The Art of Perseverance*. New York: Penguin Group, 2006.

Burns, Bob. *Recovery From Divorce: How to Become Whole Again After the Devastation of Divorce*. Tennessee: Oliver-Nelson Books, 1989.

Frydenger, Tom & Adrienne. *The Blended Family*. Michigan: Baker House, 1984.

Allender, Dan B. and Longmen III, Tremper. *Bold Love*. Colorado: Navpress, 1992.

Bevere, John, *Breaking Intimidation: How to Overcome Fear and Release the Gifts of God in Your Life*. Florida: Creation House, 1995.

Hybels, Bill, *Courageous Leadership*. MIchigan: Zondervan, 2002.

Severe, Sal. *How to Behave So Your Children Will, Too!* Penguin Putnam Inc.: New York, 2000.

Eggerichs, Emerson. *Love & Respect*. Nashville: Integrity Publishers, 2004.

Mazlish, Elaine and Faber, Adele. *How To Talk So Kids Will Listen & Listen So Kids Will Talk*. New York: Avon Books, 1980.

Barnett, Tommy. *Adventure Yourself*. Florida: Creation House, 2000.

Griffin, Emilie. *Turning.* New York: Doubleday, 1982.

Harvey, Andrew. *The Way of Passion: A Celebration of Rumi.* Berkeley, CA: Frog, Ltd., 1994.

Rupp, Joyce. *The Cup of Our Life: A Guide for Spiritual Growth.* Indiana, Ave Maria Press,1997.

Warren, Rick. *The Purpose Driven Life: What On Earth Am I Here For?* Grand Rapid, Michigan: Zondervan, 2002.

Smoke, Jim. *7 Keys To A Healthy Blended Family.* Eugene, Oregon: Harvest House Publishers, 2004.

Leman, Dr. Kevin. (with Belinda Jolley). *Bringing Peace & Harmony to the Blended Family: Where Everyone Feels At Home.* Dallas, Texas: Sampson Ministry Resources, 2000.

Washington, Ned and Harline, Leigh. *When You Wish Upon a Star.* Walt Disney, 1940.